The FutureCycle Poetry Book Prize

All full-length volumes of poetry published by FutureCycle Press in a given calendar year are considered for the annual FutureCycle Poetry Book Prize. This allows us to consider each submission on its own merits, outside of the context of a contest. Too, the judges see the finished book, which will have benefitted from the beautiful book design and strong editorial gloss we are famous for.

The book ranked the best in judging is announced as the prize-winner in the subsequent year. There is no fixed monetary award; instead, the winning poet receives an honorarium of 20% of the total net royalties from all poetry books and chapbooks the press sold online in the year the winning book was published. The winner is also accorded the honor of being on the panel of judges for the next year's competition and, in this capacity, receives a copy of all books in contention for that year's prize.

About FutureCycle Press

FutureCycle Press is dedicated to publishing lasting English-language poetry books, chapbooks, and anthologies in both print-on-demand and ebook formats. Founded in 2007 by long-time independent editor/publishers and partners Diane Kistner and Robert S. King, the press incorporated as a nonprofit in 2012. A number of our editors are distinguished poets and writers in their own right, and we have been actively involved in the small press movement going back to the early seventies.

The FutureCycle Poetry Book Prize and honorarium is awarded annually for the best full-length volume of poetry we publish in a calendar year. Introduced in 2013, our Good Works projects are anthologies devoted to issues of universal significance, with all proceeds donated to a related worthy cause. Our Selected Poems series highlights contemporary poets with a substantial body of work to their credit; with this series we strive to resurrect work that has had limited distribution and is now out of print.

We are dedicated to giving all of the authors we publish the care their work deserves, making our catalog of titles the most diverse and distinguished it can be, and paying forward any earnings to fund more great books.

We've learned a few things about independent publishing over the years. We've also evolved a unique, resilient publishing model that allows us to focus mainly on vetting and preserving for posterity the most books of exceptional quality without becoming overwhelmed with bookkeeping and mailing, fundraising activities, or taxing editorial and production "bubbles." To find out more about what we are doing, come see us at www.futurecycle.org.

For Anita,
forever the sweetheart at my door

Contents

Invitation

Engagement

Ordeals of Awakening

Devotion as the Aerobics of Love

Acknowledgments

"Suddenly the drunken sweetheart appeared out of my door.
She drank a cup of ruby wine and sat by my side.
Seeing and holding the lockets of her hair
My face became all eyes, and my eyes all hands."

From *Rumi: Thief of Sleep* by Shahram Shiva

Invitation

Matinee

I remember the girls, all of them, even my young wife —
eyes awake with excited brilliance, silver dangling earrings

and fresh mouths expanding with lip stick, with explosive color,
and how, in the grunted darkness of the cinema, we'd kiss

each other, invade the small tactile spaces beneath clothing,
kneel and lead each other into temptation without even trying,

and how it was nothing, not the movie, not the geeky ushers,
not the time spell clicking off the cinema reels, could prevent us,

stop us from our auditions with each other, movie cameras
that the sexes always are with each other, and when, at closing,

when the movie sputtered to ending, to its finish, we'd hustle
up out of seats, bursting with lust, with ambition, with exertion,

lovers at the matinee, at the movie scripts of our screen plays
with each other, and we'd replay the movie still later, in the backseat

of the car, on the couch while it rained, in the unmade bed,
matinee idols that we hoped we all were, making our movies.

Sister Kathleen Ann

In the third grade
I learned about
sexual intercourse
from my teacher,
Sister Kathleen Ann,
whose face resembled
a white gardenia
blossoming out
of a blue nun's habit.
I was eight years old
and hungry to find out
how the world worked.
Especially how it was
my babysitter
could let her white face
and red lips
fall through time
and space and kiss me
softly on the cheek
so that afterwards
my belly would feel
like I was racing
downhill on a sleigh ride.
Sister Kathleen Ann
told us about sex
by telling us about
the magical arrangement
of math. Told us
Beauty came into being
through One added to Two,
which would equal Three.
Which was bigger than two.
Told us that math
was the handiwork
of the Great Mystery
through Genesis,
which was the story
of all of Creation.
Told us that Beauty,
which was like a swan
cascading across
a pond in springtime,

had no real fixed shape
or form to it,
that it was Inevitable,
and a Force at times
wholly unpredictable,
which was Creativity.
Men and Women together
had the power
of the Sun and the Earth.
They were lovers.
Beings capable of a magic
we didn't yet comprehend.
But if we learned
how the mathematics of it
added up in class,
then we could together
find a way to talk
about it with each other
and get an A grade for it.
I worried that
if Monsignor ever
found out about
Sister Kathleen Ann
telling us about sex,
she'd be pushed
out of school forever.
Monsignor would
lean across his pulpit
and shout out to us
that when God
took shape on earth
he'd wear the face
of a bearded man.
I didn't understand
the math of that.
How God could only be a man.
Especially when
Sister Kathleen Ann
would let her eyes
crinkle into sunlight
as her fingers
caressed red rose petals.
She told us about
Beauty and Love

and Separation,
which she called
Things Being Born
and Dying because
they'd lost
the ability to join.
Love was joining.
Death was letting go.
Life was the math of it.
And the Universe
above the school yard
could be a summer plate
holding all our
mysterious dreams in it.
I fell in love with
Sister Kathleen Ann —
watched the S-shaped
curve of her body
wiggling inside
her nun's habit
as she brushed past me
on the last day of class.
Drew her a picture —
of the "Sun and the Earth
sprouting Red Roses " —
when I said
goodbye to her.

The Girls at the Vista Maria Home for Truants

– for Jeff Poleno

We wait here, standing among the trees
    losing all their leaves.
        The runaway girls gather at the windows

in intimate pairs. The blonde with the hoop earrings huddles
    against the raised shoulders
        of the freckle-faced girl

stretched tight in her silver mini skirt and her tank top,
    and the brunette in fishnet stockings
        and the scar across her left cheek

nudges against the Latino girl with the crucifix tattoo
    stippled across her left wrist.
        And just for a flickering moment,

like sparkling fish that volley and swarm
    and then heave against the rock walls
        to get a better spot in the crowded throng,

the girls push back and forth together
    like eager fans at a concert.
        And they heave and sigh

and they release their waiting emotions again...
    We teenage boys, who stand outside the windows,
        tease and taunt them.

We gaze in through the cracked window panes,
    hungry eyes.
        Make gestures at the girls

to break free, come run away with us.
    We fall back together, sip our open beers
        at the side door of the '71 Gran Torino.

Later on, whispering to one of the girls
    who kneels down to blow cigarette smoke at us
        through a crack in the window pane,

along the ledge where the laundry room dryers
    whirl and burl with the swish and roll
        of drying bedsheets,

I run my fingers across the edge of glass there,
and I touch her thin finger,
our hands, merciful strangers,

finding flame.

Some Purple Violets at the Market

– for Peter Roseman

1.

Every smell is a wish of God come to stillness in the nose.
That's why I am smelling these flowers at the market
and thinking of a woman whose smell is gone forever.

You can think what you want about these flowers. Their aroma,
like fragrant women, all of them, come off a boat —
immigrant beauties tied together, like slaves, like lovers,
like a bouquet of delicate, captured lives, shorn somehow
from some larger, masculine stalk; now geishas, now wives,
now bundles of flowers in your arms at the market.
Now, finally, a pot of purple violets for your window sill.

The nose collects whatever's left of beauty.

2.

I suppose the cartographer of smells, which is the *violet angel*,
collecting and mapping all the smells of the world
is the one God made with a careless gesture of a hand
one morning, on his way through a bed of clover.
But the violet angel's fooled God — for she was born
like a lover awakened from a mix of sleepiness and lust,
for God was intent on finding himself in something else —
and I'm afraid the violet angel was quickly passed over,
a momentary pleasure on his way to a bed of roses...
I'll tell you, she has the briefest smell, this violet angel,
here at the market along with all these other flowers.
The smell's a flirtation, something tickling a nose hair...
The violet angel appears and disappears, a purple smell
at once cooked up, in a cup of sugar and amethyst.
I tell you, she's cloudsmoke, she's sugar and amethyst.
And when God left her, he twisted himself backwards
as if to chase the lavender smell, now hiding...

Fragrant violets are God's lovers, I tell you, *flirting*.

3.

And once in bed, in 1810, Josephine kissed Napoleon
on the mouth, and he smelled *violets* on her lips.
Afterwards, when they made their love, which is the way

God conveys light and life through the cells
of a man, and his lust, a rogue, finally captured him
in a bed of anguish he would never be able to touch
or finalize — because sex is where a woman collects
a man to herself, and *he's* conquered *too*, in her fragrance —
Napoleon rolled over, he was *bereft,* he belonged to her.
And after lust there's beauty, it's a violet smell
you know, on Josephine's lips, it's a scented delight
lasting just an eternal second in the nasal cavity
before we're in anguish once again; we're lonesome and aimless.
And when Josephine died, Napoleon planted a bed of violets
on her grave...

You see, the nose collects whatever's left of beauty.

Here in my arms, this pot of violets.
Here in my bed, this woman.
Here in her grave, this other woman.

4.

You don't *own* the violet angel, though.

She's inside the lit eyes of a young woman who posed
naked for you one winter night in your flat —
because you *asked* her to, so you could photograph her.
It was back then, when you were a young man confused
by God, and so the storage of everything you could
hold inside your arms seemed at once *forever* and, at once, *not.*

But greed doesn't answer the question for beauty...
Greed doesn't answer the question of how light and life unveil
between a woman and a man...

The only thing greed does isn't relevant to beauty...

Because *forever, once,* and *not* are all the same...
They're the smells of violets flaring up
and fading somewhere far off in a meadow.
You can't take them with you.
They're flaring up, receding; they're amethyst and smoke
inside the beaming smile of a young woman
sitting there on the bed, spraying her neck
with perfume after you took her picture
one winter night...because you *asked* her.

18.

And when she laughed, you thought, like God,
you had her smell, but you *didn't,* you never did.
She had yours. And didn't. It doesn't even matter.

Every smell is a wish of God come to stillness in the nose.

Even the one flower you see, crushed on the road.
Even the one lying over the coffin.

In the end the wish is always indescribable.

So is her smell. Even you.

Psych Ward

The psych ward orderlies, pulling a woman off the floor
as she curls up like a smudged potato trying to nose herself
back into the dirt, resemble the common potato harvesters
in Jean Francois Millet's noble painting, *The Gleaners,*
and the young woman, drawing all of this on her paper pad,
sketches frantically back and forth, one line at a time.
She says quickly to me, "all delusion is a struggle with form."
And the psychiatrist standing offside comments, "we
must administer more Haldol; she's hallucinating."
The gargantuan man at the window trying to reach God
extends his lethargic arm out and the playing cards drop.
At the edge of the room, a man in spectacles pages through
a book. Laughs quietly, losing his religion, and he whispers
to me that "we have angels and demons in us — they
squirm like octopi in our grinning, as if trying to take shape."
I trace my mouth with my hand, as if trying to find it.
The woman with a mole on her face shouts out that Jesus
is the example of dialectics — the struggle with opposites;
the struggle with life and death, meaning and oblivion —
and the young woman at the table scratches her right arm
with her fingernails. One of the orderlies pushes her hand away.
The young woman says, "I have a right to give up."
Sunlight shines through the cracked window panes.
The room has a pewter glow to it. Shadows hit the walls.
The tile floor below us resembles a spilled pot of beef stew.
The man points to my grin, says, "you see the human smile
is a twisted tabernacle; it's the joke God made in us
so that we show who we really are to each other whenever
we grin." That our smiles could contain a node of angels
and demons is taken up by the psychiatric residents:
"I feel so revealed," a woman says, and the other, a man,
whispers, "let's get a drink afterwards," and the woman
who is revealed pauses, grins, steps back behind the
psychiatrist, who says, "psychopathology is the revealing
of a brain disorder; it's medically treatable." A man pounds
on the table, shouts out that there are bugs crawling
up his arms and shoos them all off; and the residents, piling
together in a batch, cluster around him to look.
"Disease is an amalgamation of misinformed thoughts,"
says the psychiatrist, pointing at the man with bugs
invading his arms and his neck, and I feel the tongue
in my mouth as it moves, suddenly, like a squid.

I can't tell whether I have a tongue anymore or a squid.
"Doubt is the attempt to regain perspective," he adds,
pointing to the lack of doubt — the delusion. The man
in the spectacles laughs again, points to his half grin,
and announces to the room that "we're just creatures
of deception at all times, and it's about time to admit it —
we can't even tell the soul from the source..." and he squawks.
The residents act bewildered, look around at each other.
And the psychiatrist informs them that uncertainty
isn't something worth getting caught in, in psychiatry.
"Medicine is the enactment of a cure," he reassures them,
"even if it is inexact for a while." I step closer,
stand alongside the woman who is still sketching.
She's drawn the gleaners. She says to me, "information
comes from uncertainty, don't you think?" And she
smiles sheepishly, and I can't tell if the smile has an angel
or a demon in it. The psychiatrist reassures the residents
that "the cure is when a person recognizes reality again."
I feel the squid in my mouth move around, and my smile
feels like it's wrapped around two squirrels fighting.
The young woman scratching herself fights on. "I have
a right to give up," she announces again to the sunlight.
The psychiatrist looks at her and he rubs his chin.
Scribbles something on a prescription pad. Hands it off.
"What about the imagination?" asks a resident, puzzled.
"That's something for art," the psychiatrist answers.
"And science, and religion," he adds, "but not for us."
And they all turn and depart the room in a brawl.
The woman drawing on her sketch pad rotates it,
rotates it again, as if trying to find herself inside it.

Woman Releasing a Tongueless Swallow from Her Violin

1.

Because I am sad-Irish, I hear the screams of the swallow above me, her tonguelessness in every woman I meet, in the way they become speechless.

And because I've grown frightened for the swallow in every woman's throat, its voice a mixture of screech and saw mill scratching, its ecstasy

so bold as it rises and falls out of chimneys and cold utterings, I listen, always, for the song of the violin on any city street, the violin being

the heart's larynx. I see them here, these two young women, busking outside a Starbucks in Pike Place Market, the one hoisting her violin

up to the blue sky bursting with deafening sea gulls, and the second one, straddling a wooden box, ripping on a saw, making it moan. Look here

at this woman in her black dress, hair pinned up, fish net stockings, her polka-dotted top, her eyes raised up to the sun, fiddling on her violin,

releasing from catgut strings the Irish Swallow Tail Jig.

2.

And once, when I was alone in the market, shopping for simple fruit, I saw a woman struck by her husband. It was almost delicate, the practiced

deliberation, the care in his back hand as he met her cheek, and in slow mode she stumbled backwards, away from him into the produce bin,

where he caught her in his extended, outstretched arm, like they were tangoing, the apples bobbling behind them in their rows, as he languidly

scooped one up to give to her — the violence we do with each other being intimate, being the way we cripple each other in our need — and, as she was

caught by his strong arm, her little mouth opened up in fright, her teeth biting the small bird which was her tongue, the swallow in her mouth,

from her throat came a voiceless screech, the swallow song escaping her along with all the other swallows dipping and forking out of the open shoulders of the brick buildings of the market on that sunny summer day, while a solitary violinist, someone hidden from view and fiddling behind

the broken, fetid crates of fruits and vegetables, played a jig while the rest of us, gathered here at the market, shopped for food. And as I heard it,

I heard it as the Irish "Swallow Tail Jig."

3.

And so here, in Pike Place Market — along with the women in purple coats, chestnut scarves covering pale throats, their slender shoulders winged —

I listen for the violin squirming inside the tongueless mouth of the swallow, setting the jig free so that it swoops down and up the street in ecstasy...

I listen to the woman with a yellow flower in her hair fiddling away on her violin, while the other woman moans away on her box saw. They play for

us, so that the tongueless swallow — the tongue sliced out of its pinched mouth by a god so vengeful he'd slay his own kin in order to take into bed

the innocent girl with the one song in her mouth and her voice so hidden — can find her freedom to sing again. The tongue of a woman being a holy

trope: all songs for the violin being for the tongueless women among us who've forgotten how very beautiful they sing, or have longed to raise voice

to linger, or have yelped, of fiddled voice in sorrow, felt skin tingle under caress of finger or have been punished in the very act of doing it, all women

being free, being lovely swallows, that sing.

Pictures

There you are on the bed, curled up, legs
crossed languidly like rope sensually braiding
itself, reading your book about photography
in the 20th Century, in the city landscape,
the cashmere sweater robed around your
body, holding the whiteness of it in, lips
red, the soul-blood of you, pure as flowers,
and pearls spilled down into your cleavage
making you resemble a concubine out
of Manet, one of his models stretched out
on a divan, ready for the painting; and here's *me,*
standing over you, my quick instant camera
in hand, snapshots while we are young.
Your smile, an enterprise of bright light.
You think this was years ago. No, it was
just last week, and the plum trees were full
in bloom, the birds hiding there in pines
were out of breath with singing, the street
noisy with children riding their bicycles,
all the world around us crazy with spring.
Even the neighborhood, so quiet all winter,
had come to life again. People, faces pale
as turnips, coming out to say hello again,
the root tubers of people, men and women
stretched alongside open doorways, talking,
drinks in hand, cigarettes dangling, laughing.
And the Polish man with foreboding in his
eyes sitting there on his porch, smoking,
talking to himself again about Krakow,
about a life there, and a woman planting
a garden full of red and white flowers,
her eyes wide awake with swallows.
You, there on the bed, a bouquet nude.
"The voice of a man, you ask? It is a broken
string full of unbearable literature." This is
what he would tell me as I drank there
in the dense summer evenings with him.
"And a woman, you ask, she is a salvation, *yes?*"
She is the richness of the upturned earth,
her eyes wide awake with sudden swallows.

"She is your garden, *yes?*" A smile on his lips.
"She is your earthly delight, yes, your, how
do you say it, *pearly everlasting,* and you
are the light, what she will see of herself, *yes?*
Take pictures of her," he said to me, his eyes
mixed and incongruent, foreboding, dark.
The dangling arms stretched over legs,
blue squiggly numbers inked there on his wrists.
Eyes the color of coal in outdoor ovens.
"You are young once, just once," raising
the liquor to his opened mouth, sipping it.
Me, lighting up another cigarette for him.
"Take many pictures of her, *many,*" he said.
"The world is rabid, yes, but it is good,
it is always good, and hungry just once,
your gut so tense with the hunger of it,
and your wife, yes? She is, how do you say it,
enchanted?" Yes, she is that word, *that,* yes.

My Fingers Move Across the Typewriter Keys in an Effort to Find You

because I am hungry and desirous of you, woman
with the stars across your belly, necklace of pearls,

but the man with the thin mustache and the long
ebony cane is standing here in the doorway with us

again, a black rose in his lapel and, underneath his arm,
that book of Romanian poetry, that anthology,

and he is reading it out loud again to us —
to the both of us as we sit here quietly,

legs folded on the unmade bed before making love
as visitors in this lonesome city we've never been to

until just now, the opened bottle of wine half gone,
the dark color of it resting low in glasses

like raspberry moons that have somehow capsized
out of the dark night sky, into these open glasses,

as the silent, last walkers beat the dusk down
on their way back home from the open markets

to their own dinner tables, sleeper dreamers
that we all are. And he says to us, paging through

the book, that the world is either a joyful fountain
spiking water up, or else it is a mound of earth,

stagnant with yellow flowers shriveled in spring.
And we listen to his mouth, a thin moving lizard,

as he reads each and every line from a poem called
"The Sleeper Dreamers Wake Up in Their Bodies,"

and one of the lines says that "my fingers move
across the typewriter keys in an effort to find you

asleep in your desire, here in the aftermath
of someone you've forgotten, some dream

where you are aghast in pearls by a cracked tree —
unsure of your beauty because you are *silenced*."

"Do you hear that," he says, "the poet writes that we
are silenced, first and foremost, like mimes

with each other when we fall into estrangement
and grace with each other, eyes locked in need,

muted lovers that we are, seeking each other's light."
And he reads to us that to fall in love is to collapse

into the influence of the *erotic*. "Do you hear it, lovers,"
he reads to us, "it is to fall dizzily into the influence

of the erotic," which is the open hand of our reaching.
As if all those of us who would run our spidered

fingers across the wonders of a body in a bed,
in a hotel by a wandering dark river, would come first,

mute and erotic, like silent mimes bearing witness
to each other, only to discover we're just encoded light

streaming into each other's bodies when we make love.
We're just light seeking a source. Because the fingers,

mine, the poet says, *are* silent mimes spilling themselves
over each letter of your body, voluptuous alphabet

that it is, beautiful template of groans and silences.
And we find out who we are, he says, leaving us to finish

up with each other, lovers in our intimate last moments
together, in the quick spike and release of rapture.

"Revealed too, we are," he says, shutting the book
of poetry, leaving us "in the unknown roaming

willingness of it all," sleeper dreamers that we are,
touching each other in any city, a strange man reading

poetry to us.

Three-Birds Orchid

"Among the graffiti one illuminated name: yours"
— Basho

Poised in beauty at the woozy edge
    of this drunken swamp,
        a mile deep into woods

like an enchanted pilgrim silently
    climbing the ambrosial pathway
        to heaven's gate,

you startle me
    with your earnest meditation,
        oh sweet Buddhist orchid,

oh soft demented flora,
    oh silent saint of contemplation,
        oh sweet honey flower

of woodland mystery. I come upon you
    growing here in this heap
        of leaves and rotting humus

like a floral spit of liquid sculpture
    rising elegantly
        from the omphalos of dirt.

You remind me of my wife
    as she ascended the stairway
        of her youth

into the bridal registry
    of her womanhood,
        a stem of buds awakening her,

some painted white and purple,
    a cough of feathers inside her,
        a vase of flowers.

You remind me
    of myself as I have risen,
        lonesome and flummoxed

in the drunkenness of my evenings,
    worry and woe twisted
        tight around my temples

as if I am still the bewildered groom
      approaching my lover
           with vanishing at my core,

something panicked and hopeful
      inside my belly,
           a graft of flying birds.

You remind me
      of an altar of *sylphs,*
           colorful spirits of the air

promising not security, not seduction,
      nothing at all except for
           being, expanding...

And erupting
      from your saint-stem,
           three pink-and-white

orchid birds — I see them —
      freeing themselves
           in lopsided,

emancipated flight,
      as if enflaming themselves
           up through the squalid air,

in majesty, from the woven collar
      of each sunburst axil,
           each cradle of becoming,

as if the body, ours,
      emaciated
           like an orchid stem

with hunger, with vanishing,
      could actually
           bloom and exhale

winged beings,
      three-bird orchids —
           me, you, and *us*

from the aroused
      unfolding of its
           reaching,

right here at the edge of a swamp
      in the woods,
           just because.

Reading Jean Piaget w/Margo

She holds a branch of foliage in her hand. She detaches the leaves
and throws them to the ground one by one. Each time she very carefully
explores the trajectory. The same day she alternately moves a strainer
away from her and brings it toward her.
— Jean Piaget, 1954

And then a beam of afternoon light invades
the room where he is studying this girl,
Jean Piaget, who would later tell what it is
that's happening when a little girl awakens
within the sharp clarity of consciousness
and discovers her father sitting there beside her.
Nothing else is being born yet. Only me,
myself, studying this field of displacements.
Crossing and uncrossing my legs in the late
September warmth on a Tuesday afternoon.
The me and the not me, working forwards and
backwards between the terminals of selfhood,
as I learn that a child's father is just one of the
objects of displacement a child sees, becomes
a part of, comes close to or parts with, or not.
And so I reach out and grab her, pull her soft
cheeks to mine, and I kiss them till she wiggles
apart again and throws herself to the leaves.
And then I feel full again, I belong to her again,
which makes my eyes squint, as if to see her,
or me, or whatever else exists in the field of
father and daughter becoming father with daughter.
Nothing else is being born yet. Only her and me
and the full afternoon light that's disguising the
future, which is, I presume, the light rays of
the everything she's going to fly into — her life,
one day — quicker than I know it.

On Highway 90, in South Dakota, Margo & I See in the End What We Become

— for Margo

Each morning for a month he would sketch
the gray doe stampeding across the highway
somewhere in the middle of South Dakota
on the trip out west to Seattle, Washington,
just before the small compact car rammed it good
as the driver swerved away toward the inner brim
of the highway, nearly killing it on the spot.
He would draw to scale the woman's head
as she swerved. He'd draw her man, asleep beside her,
jumping up frightened by the twist and smack of it,
and how the doe had catapulted head over heart
and back, before being reborn in a dead-run jump
across the rancher's fence, where it had escaped
with its mate who had jumped ahead.
How in the instant there was the strange light
where time had stopped to take a look:
How in a quick frame he saw the way we *leave* —
from where we've come from to what we are.
He would say to his daughter in a poem, "I can't
get it out of my head the way the doe in flight
became a violin, opening up."

Engagement

My Wedding

My wedding was a fish. It roused itself awake
by leaping out of calm water.
It flip-flopped all over the grass
on a steamy August morning in 1988.
Rows and rows of guests poured cool water on it.
Bagpipes made its eyes bug out.
My wife entered the fish by its mouth,
led down the hatch by her father.
I lingered by the rib cage, watching
her gliding towards me like a white feather,
a beautiful swan's feather suddenly
coughed out of girlhood.
All girls are born behind the large wings of a bird.
Some are dark wings. Some gray.
Some girls start out dirty as oil and end up that way.
Some are fresh as porcelain.
The sun shone in slender beams
through the fish's eyes.
I swear it seemed more like a chapel.
The reverend helped us sew our vows together,
and we were strung together.
Dancing made us elastic. We stretched.
We made noise. I am a man.
All men are born broken as the seal
is first broken on wads of money.
They are soiled taproots.
No man can repair what is first broken.
A wedding ceremony is a healing.
I danced until I felt as lost as a planet's moon.
I shivered behind sweat. My wife
heard the tiny bells in her nipples ringing.
She shimmied down to grab the garter
from my knee. Background music
consisted of the future. Every wedding
has an uninvited guest called the future.
I looked for the future in a bathroom mirror,
but it refused to be visible.
The music was as loud as water in a bathtub.
I felt the fish trying to dive.
Every wedding is a crying out of strange noises.
That night we cried out our darkness
in a bed in Leamington, Ontario.

A Bouquet of Roses at the Market Leading into Afternoon Sex

I remember:

Stalks and stalks of roses, slender and voluptuous, wavering in a white pail,
here at the spring flower market, all of them for sale, a *Chorus Memoire*

of my sexual desire: *April in Paris, Pink Promise, Cherries in Cream*, tea roses,
ramblers, climbers; and Queen Anne's lace clinging like silk bridal tulle lace

shivering at rose stem throats, lovely brides that these fresh roses are —
bold, awaiting their wedding engagement, their sale. And us, gathered here,

gazing down upon them. You, flirting with me, pressing your body to me secretly,
so that no one will see, and then, lifting one of the red roses up

to show me its unique sex: its opened, bursting blossom revealed by heat,
by lust, and heralded forth by an erotic desire, by a libidinous willingness,

in a kind of exhibitionism to show me itself: its skin and its petal folds:
as if the rose, because of its arousal, its *sexual play*, its "Stairway to Heaven"

could be the romp of the new bride and groom, of Adonis and Aphrodite
in flirtatious sexual foreplay, like us.

Learning to Taste the Chocolate

After making love with my wife on a Sunday morning,
she tells me that we can't have sex for a whole month.
"Let's see if you can wait that long without bugging me
about it so much," she advises me. "You've been bugging me
about it too much, like you're obsessed with it, the sex,
and not *me*," she tells me, pulling my face closer to hers,
her eyes blazing but not angry, more like completely convinced.
The small blinking of her eyes convincing me too.
"And I'm more important than what you want from me,
no matter what," she adds over her shoulder, while hauling
the dirty laundry down the stairs for washing, whistling as she goes.
I'm still wrapped in the bed sheets, still there after the lovemaking,
still in the afterglow of it, and wondering how I'll actually wait
a month for sex. I wonder how I'll possibly wait it out that long.
I watch a bird poking around for stray seeds in the window box
outside the bedroom window. Let my hand roam across
my face and then down my neck and then down onto my chest.
I wonder if she ever actually thinks about my body in that lusty,
out-of-control way that I dream of her body. The smoothness
of her neck and the cut of her cleavage, the crease of her thighs
in a summer skirt. She shows up again, suddenly, a box
of chocolate candy in her left hand, grinning at me. Curls up
beside me on the bed, opens the box. Gently takes my chin
in her hand and she opens my mouth. Feeds me one chocolate
at a time, tells me to take one bite, "just one," she says, "and then
go ahead and toss it away, over there," she insists.
And she bites one too, tosses it, tells me, "take one bite —
and that's all, so you learn to taste the chocolate, then let it go."

Forgiving

After the fight, which was like a telephone
call between both of them and no one
answering it rightly, they got into the old Jeep
and drove to a corner bar. Ordered a few drinks.
Jumbo shrimp and sauce. French fries. Ketchup.
She told him she'd never ever forgive him
for saying her ass was getting fat as his mother's.
And that he could forget about sex, it was
pretty much off the table like a spilled drink.
Said that the arguing had to stop once and for all,
and that it felt like stones hitting her on her face
all the time, and she couldn't get out of the way
of it any more without really starting to hate him.
She ate another shrimp. Wiped her nose off
with a napkin and also her eye. Said, "I'm not
crying." He said, "I know it. I'm not thinking it."
He said he didn't really care about sex with her
so long as she'd let him sleep in the bed beside her
on account that it was winter and they still
hadn't bought the big comforter she'd seen
on sale last Sunday in the JCPenny catalogue.
She looked at him like he was a cold dog trying
to get back in the bedroom even though the rule
was he was to sleep most nights in the doghouse.
She said only if he said he was sorry for calling
her a fat ass and if he'd let the cat sleep on the bed
like she'd been wanting since last fall when it
got cold and the cat turned 14. He said okay
and fed her the last jumbo shrimp, said it's
only fair, "I had four, you only had three."
Then he apologized for calling her a fat ass.
Even wiped her chin off with his finger and thumb.
Gently, like he was stroking the chin of the cat.
She said okay. The waiter came over to their table,
asked them if they wanted more drinks, food.
She said no, he said yes, and she said, okay, and that
was that.

Adolescence

We were quarreling and she said to me
"you push when you should receive,
it's probably something from your
adolescence hanging around somehow."
The cats had gathered there on the bed
to watch us, and the summer breezes
shook the curtains and enflamed them
with air so that when they rose and fell
they were like dancers. Our daughter
stood there rocking on the street curb,
talking to a new boy. She was about to take
the leap that all girls take when their skin
changes, and suddenly the stirring of their
deepermost feelings, which sit safely
locked underneath the compress of skin
for years, emerge somehow as wildflowers
or a sudden rain storm of giggles, and then
everything is different, alive somehow,
like an unleashed current of passion.
She said to me, "don't ruin it for her."
That meant she was going to tell me
that I was a failure at feelings. And she said,
"I know what you're thinking, which is
another mistake. It's more of your nonsense."
And she stroked my arm again, gently,
like it was asleep or something.
"Pain is your exit wound. The boat
that always sits there, waiting; *it's waiting
for you*. Do you know that?" she asked.
"Do you know that it's waiting? Just
give it up. Give it away." And then she lifted
up the front of my shirt, ran her finger
down me. Once, twice, like she was
unstitching and then sewing something
up on my exposed chest. Her finger
felt like a golden velvet tip. Something
warmed and familiar. Something soothing.
And she turned my head again to look out
the window at the boy and the girl.
I watched the girl on the street curb

talking to the boy who was practicing
what it felt like to let a girl feel her feelings
toward him. He grinned, curled one
sandal over the other one, coyly almost,
and he let her come close to him —
to fluff his hair — and he let his head
rise up to show her his young neck,
vulnerable and tanned with the sunlight,
so she could kiss it.

Love (The Drunken Sweetheart at My Door)

Because I have sadness like a plum
     in my fatted heart,
         and because you

are trying your wild strawberry-shaped heart
     on for size with me
         to show me something of yourself,

to show me that we're merely
     numerical variations with each other
         at all times,

just zeros and ones with each other
     as part of the formula we use
         to complete each other,

we kiss out here on this rock overlooking
     the Atlantic as the seagulls toss themselves
         into wind.

And because love is the drunken sweetheart
     at my door, I awaken alive
         in my desire for you,

to give to you all the days of my heart's journey,
     all the devotion and devastation
         in my soul,

and I give to you all the doorways
     in and out of it, all the passageways
         no matter the hour,

which is love's religion. And you risk everything
     by unbuttoning your blouse
         out here in the blue wind

and I slide in next to you
     and I undo your dress
         so that we can consume

each other again,
     here on our honeymoon
         in Nova Scotia.

And because you kiss with fervent ease,
     and because I am a falling rock,
         I fall down

over the edge of cliff stone, grabbing in hand
      a tuft of simple flowers
            as I fall into deep sea.

And because you are there,
      you take hold of my hips again
            and yank me into you —

kissing me, pulling me back in again
      to your strawberry mouth,
            pulling me back in again,

exchanging your drunken sweetheart
      with me again, over and over again,
            which is love.

Empathy

The red blood on your forehead
    after you tripped and fell on
        the oceanside trail
           on our honeymoon

trickled down over your eyelid,
    blinding you momentarily
        so that you couldn't see.

Above us, seagulls gossiped over the cliffs
    above the wavy ocean,
        and the grasses waved back
           and forth in windy rhyme

so that I couldn't hear you cry out, call out for me,
    for I'd walked well ahead of you, out of your sight,
        was all the way to a rock,

had grown inpatient with the pace you'd set
    as you started and stopped, picked flowers,
        pointed out the ocean bird's
           shivering wing on wind,

and I'd fallen into reverie, was pacing myself
    against the rip of wind and sun, against
        the slower wade and walk of us together.

Then something in me was arrested,
    was stopped in my tracks. I could feel
        that you couldn't see me;
           my body simply felt it,

and I jerked backwards, saw you sitting there,
    the world around you crowding your shape,
        you, stiffened there in pain,

and I ran back to you, startled, my legs pumping,
    pushing forward, stuffing wind behind them,
        so that I nearly fell on you,
           so afraid for you, with you.

And you looked up, your eyes racing for me —
    into me, into my empathy —
        quick and present, like the wind.

Twin Flame

When we had sex together that first time
in my bed, in that turn-of-the-century
apartment in Detroit, the two of us
dazed, breathless, our arms wrapped
tightly around one another like we'd
become one bird on fire flying into itself —
feathers and flame for the first time
as the police sirens outdoors wailed
one after the other in hot pursuit
of something neither one of us could see —
I stretched my shoulders wide as if spreading
the deepest bones in my back aflutter,
like fanning some kind of alleluia awake.
And when I bent down to look at you
and you turned your face up to me
like we we'd become one flame in mid-spiral —
lost somehow in feathers and flight,
in swirling blue flame and hot breath —
I saw that sex was one of the catalyst dances
where love's made inside a twin flame.
And when we were finished, I saw
the thin skin of your eyelids blinking on
and off like the delicate wings of a bird
opening and closing on the furnace of your
Being, until you sealed the air in your lungs
from the wanting of me and the taking
of me, and you inhaled deep into your lungs
again and exhaled — the perfume of
you spreading flush against my hot cheeks
and into my nostrils — and I remembered
that the shape of flame rising from fire
could lift it up high and erratic again,
ceaselessly here and gone in its seeking,
in the strange polygamy of its leaping,
in this fulcrum of inhale and ecstasy,
in this falling back into each other as sex.
And then you looked up at me again
and you blew, and blew again on me,
and I knew then that in each other's
flame in sex was the smoke of the one
flowing back into the many, and the
many flowing back in again to the one.

Concerning the Metaphysics of My Wife's Otherness

The angels, stretching their bluegum eucalyptus bodies against the ordinary
background of the mirror I'm standing in, aren't ordinary. They are,

to quote the physicist Arthur Eddington, "smeared all over a probability
distribution," just as my wife who's standing at the vanity mirror

distributing the California fuchsia lipstick across her soft lips
is also just herself a theoretical construct — not quite reality substance,

not quite wave-spell — that I find myself involved in. We are about
to celebrate our wedding anniversary. We've just found ourselves

in love again, our hands all over each other in the bed, our mouths
like hungry clams so full of greed and insistence — how the body itself

is tangled in a contest of what is verifiable and what is claimed as not.
I watch her, and I hear myself saying "junonia volute caressed in B minor,"

hear myself saying "pearly everlasting against a swathe of violin strings,"
hear the diminishing chords and the slipstream where the bow of the violin

intersects through me, through my bony clavicle and down to where
all my groin thunder is, before the music source invades and leaves me wild

and entangled in her physical beauty again, watch her as she widens
her eyes to find the woman she believes herself to be tonight —

that otherness in her that seems to me to be an ensemble
of changeable motion, a transcendent elaboration with continuity,

an essence of violins and vibrato, and not as any one woman
I can ever know.

She Was Caressing Me

— for Dorit Silver

She was caressing me, I'm quite sure of it now,
though it doesn't make any sense to me
that a strange woman from the room next door to me
would suddenly slide the curtain open and climb
into the bed with me for some purpose I couldn't see.
And the milky way of stars across my body,
on my legs and stomach, on my chest, had *opened* —
I was a felled tree lying there just breaking open.
I'm telling you this happened to me. It's all true.
I was a broken tree filled with blinking opened eyes.
All across my body were hordes of opened eyes.
This was in a hospital. I was nineteen years old
and I'd just had leg surgery, and my legs were
solid logs with their bark ripped open by surgeons.
My whole body was a tree wrapped in bandages
and so much after-blood. She'd crawled up in bed
with me, her own hospital gown covering her body,
which was thin and bony, like a California
laurel tree. And her thin hands were touching
the places on my skin where I was ripped open,
or I'd thickened over with the coarse resin of trauma.
The dusk had grabbed light. It was a black window.
The dark was invading the room and closing it.
And together we lay there, wounded, healing,
all the opened eyes on my body, on my legs
and all across my sheltered heart, on my neck
and on my belly, and even in my groin, could see.

The Wildest Girls

— for Anita

When I was a younger kid, I loved the wildest girls.
Girls who wore their buffet hearts like crème de menthe
on their sleeves, were first to French kiss me at the door,
would take my shivering face and grab it inside
their mitts, would blow heat at me through their lips.
Girls who let the planets, like Venus, enter their eyes,
wore mascara and lipstick at the roller skating parties
and short pants so that even the fathers looked back.
These were the kinds of girls that church priests
turned their black bibles on, stern nuns scolded loudly.
Girls whose hands, roaming fish, found the secrets
below my belly, whose moist mouths eagerly found
mine at the summer-night gatherings and, high on music
or on the cheap wine that we drank, let their minds
be lifted away from all care and restraint, so they
could slip sideways, like untethered boats, and become
lost in the harbor with me. Now that I am this age
and I know that the bulging heart in me still requires
excitement and a kind of fanfare to move it, I still love
the wildest girls, now grown-up women in pumps,
now wives to other men, or single lovers, or mothers
who remain chicks that doll up in fragrance and pearls.
These are the women I talk to while grocery shopping.
These are the ones chatting on cell phones in aisles,
who enchant their kids with tasty treats and kisses,
who get down on their knees, rub cheeks with their pets.
I love these kinds of women who are guided by fanfare.
Those who've let their heart's loving cup guide them,
coax them into the spunkiness of their sexual charms.
I love these kinds of women who carry no bitters —
those who bear-hug the fresh-cut bouquet of red roses,
their grocery bags collapsing underneath sandals,
their apricot grins big and lusty, full of the afternoon's
sin.

Ordeals of Awakening

I Am Not the Composer of Poetic Reverie Anymore

— Robert Schumann to Clara Wieck

he said to her, sitting with her along the simple fountain
in the aftermath of the war. "And you are not the red rose
anymore. You are not, shall I say it, in your *light skirts*
anymore like you once were outside the speakeasy where
the *pink pants,* the young homosexuals, used to cruise
each other, violins in hand, lips frosted and glittered
like ghosted, young anorexics, noses full of pimp dust.
For we are orphaned now from the stronger age, robust
as it was, auricular hallucinations of music in otherwise
deaf ears and eager hearts, so enunciated, and now
we are independent of it all, we are free." And her, "I see it."
And him, "the buildings — look around us — the library
and the music hall and the *Café Traumerei No. 7* are collapsed,
they are architectural dust, their steps are ruined."
The wind blew and so they stepped backwards, together,
into a foyer of an old hotel, sat down on a dusty couch
full of plaster, chinks of the ceiling, chandelier glass.
Him to her, "we are extinguished but free, we're nothing —
but an occasional reminiscence is preferable to desperate
independence," and he held his face in his hand, hiding it,
felt the darkness come over him, take him by the ears.
She looked hard at him, trying to find his eyes, said
"it's going to rain — do you feel it?" and him, "yes, at my
temples I feel it, in my elbows too and down, along
my sides." Beside them, outside a building whose façade
had blown open like a face, a man, a Nigerian, sold
crack cocaine in small, easy-to-open packets and a girl,
someone not any older than fifteen, a young-lady flower,
stood languidly on the half-collapsed steps, waiting,
a camellia in her hair. "Far off," he said to her, "can you
hear it, the polka someone's playing on the rugby field?"
and her, "I am a shadow, don't leave me," and him, "you
are the leaf" (touching her on the arm now, caressing it,
her arm), "you are the leaf, music the wind, I shall leave you."

Strip Clubs, Tampa

Everyone has a story,
even the woman dancing here
in front of me, fully undressed,
and waving herself like a palm tree
in front of my face
at a strip club in Tampa,
way back in 1983,
while the music thundered
through the booths like a flood.
Can you believe it?
So I asked her to quit the lap dance,
and not to do anything else,
but simply to tell me
how it came to be *this* —
if there was an answer, it fell
into reasons
that have more to do with
the economics of love
and how and where it is lost
or found in the eyes
of, say, her father, or her brother,
or her first-time lover
and less to do with money
for college, or for the trip to LA,
although she didn't want
me to know this,
and, besides, it was for cash
and for the black eye
she once earned for speaking up.
And it was for the aggression
that she felt in her belly
when she saw the men squirm
and want her
and pay for her time
like she was the goddess Shakti,
dancing here on Nevada Avenue
in Tampa Bay, Florida.
And, if all this wasn't reason
enough, there was also her
younger sister, who was raped
and pregnant,

and there was also the reason
she gave which had less
to do with sociology,
or broken dreams,
or psychology and all of its
subterranean motives,
but more to do, she figured,
with passing the time
before the lights of the bay
dropped to their hard core;
and, alone in her silence,
she could wonder how it is
dreams get lost in the crab traps
of our small unraveled lives
and end up here,
on another lit stage,
in the limelight of men's lust,
or misbegotten affections,
or mishandled attention,
and then finally end here with *me,*
a guy asking her questions
that she said *everyone* asked her.
And, whose answers,
like a handful of raw oysters,
get misplaced somewhere
under the water,
perhaps in a bed of fish hooks
or collapsed pilings,
and so she could never
really answer why.
"It doesn't matter to *anyone,"*
is all she could say.
Some nights, afterwards,
you'd see them gathering
in a circle, giggling,
as if they were school girls,
before the pressure to dance
consumed them.
And you'd wonder
what kind of young girls
they were before the thongs
and the wine coolers
and the hot little panties

stuffed with wads of cash
filled their personalities up,
way back in the days
before the silver nipples
and the nightly ritual
of rubbing ice on them
cooled their breasts
and also their hopes for true love.
And you'd wonder what
it was they'd once
wished for in their beds,
before the stripping naked
for us
chilled their sweet hearts.

Some Young Men Undressing

Women undressing is a picture that people
keep talking about in advertising ads
and in movies and in poems and songs. You never
hear about young men undressing, one by one,
like muscular, virile sculptural chordworks
standing around each other, taught as storks,
unsure of themselves at first because they are not
used to this kind of ritual, because it doesn't exist
in advertising or in poetry or in radio songs.
And one of them, lifting his left leg and ankle
out of a pair of slacks and letting the pants leg fall,
and the other not yet quite close enough to catch it
unsettled, to the floor. And you never hear
of one man helping another man out of his shirt.
Can you imagine it, the one behind the other
whispering, here, give it to me, your left shoulder.
And let me pull the one long muscular left arm
out of the left sleeve of the striped work shirt.
And the tie, still dangling from the senseless shirt.
And the one half-undressed man, letting his head
fall back, like a southern love song, onto the other
man's right shoulder, and their arms across
each other, for balance. Their ankles entwined.
It is too dangerous to think on these things.
But can you imagine it, back in the 1400s,
when art was trying to break out of its doldrums.
And the impatient young model and the painter.
The older man of the two here to do his art
with the younger man, the model. And the older
disrobing him, letting the robe fall like a dozen
red or purple roses to the floor, in a heap.
And then the painter stripping the model down
to nothing, so that the skin, opulent and tense,
can be painted, then hidden away, and never
be put into an advertisement, or a poem, or a song.

1991 at the Movies

This is 1991, and it is the year the boxer
Mike Tyson, possessed by the Devil's furies,
rapes a beauty pageant contestant
in the city of Indianapolis, and he's later
convicted to jail time. This is also the year
that the LA police beat Rodney King 56 times
in a police video and the fire sticks are lit,
deep in the fire pit, for a riot, which erupts
out of timbers by the next April. This is also
the year you see how heartbreak forms
inside the smile of a woman's face, even though
she's trying her best to lie to you and deny it.
And you figure she's trying to hide it because
she's doing her best to protect a better picture
of you, even though you're beyond deserving it.
This is during the autumn, when the leaves
are flirting with their diminishing, and the
girls walking home from school look like ripe
strings of fruit on long, giggling branches.
This is when you first hear the bird caught
in the rafters of your garage and, reaching up
through the humid darkness there, you see
that it's really only half a bird — the other half
being torn by something, a cat, a raccoon.
And you figure some things are too far gone to matter.
You don't bother with any of this, and you tell
no one. You sit for long hours in the first chill
of autumn — talking to no one, not even to her —
and you come to believe you are as lonely
as an iceberg. She stands on the stoop, watching
you, though she's quiet as the moon in the cedars.
You remember hearing the loud, violent quarrels
of a couple one night years before this
and, drunk on your own misery, you stomped
on the floor as if trying to drive them out
of their living room, as if trying to drive them
out onto the street like wild hyenas. You
remember that the woman's name was Sophie,
and she had that miserable look women wear
like a knife blade in the crook of their eyes

when they are looking right through you,
right into the soiled heart of your cruelest motives
toward them, and you figure you can't blame
them for this. And you remember that her
man was hairy and dull and uninvolved,
as if his brain had collapsed into a pile of rage.
And you remember that his shouting sounded
like a boy being beaten with a sharp stick.
And you can tell that their sexual union's more
about repeating a fight long ago started
between two or four other people no longer
part of this evening's film. And you spend
long hours whittling a walking stick for next summer,
thinking that walking will get you away
from all of this. And when she walks past you,
she looks into your eyes the way you look
into the garage at those rafters, as if she's
trying to find something inside of you,
some small spectacle of your interest in her.
You figure the trouble started between you and her
after a party where you let another woman
seduce you, although it was innocent enough:
nothing happened, nobody took anybody to bed.
It was just the power of innuendo, something
closer to trespassing than to true robbery,
though you know she thinks of it as theft.
And you know that she thinks of it as a betrayal
of some small, tender trust you can't even imagine.
And you figure that cruelty, like a hawk's claw,
sits in the middle of our desires for each other,
and you bring it with you like an unopened gift
from the wedding night, and one way or another
it gets unwrapped during sex or quarreling.
And there's no way around this but through it,
even though it cuts everything you care about
like a razor blade, or like a knife across a pillow.
And you spend long evenings by yourself,
drinking a tumbler of something on ice
and listening to the low hum of produce trucks
streaming their rage across the highways,
which is your second best plan for resolving
things. This is also the year you learn that

a woman nursing a broken heart burrows
herself into secrets more remote than heaven
or Graceland, and it's the first year you learn
that an aching heart is like a soft pillow
existing between two people, and no matter
how you care for it, you cut it, you mend it.

My Wife & I

My wife is a rhythmic meridian
    I am allowed to cross.
        She is fixed there on the bow string

of the fiddle of beauty. She is the fiddle string of beauty
    as all girls are once they break off
        the axis mundi tree

where girls are rhythmic loops of expression
    and then emotional violas
        with lipstick and tits that fool us.

Lips are beauty accessories
    on the meridian lines of mystery.
        Boys don't know how to fly kites

in the meridian lines.
    Punching each other as sublimation doesn't help
        doesn't graze beauty well.

        Nor do the horses they ride

against the feminine sky —
    which is the meridian line I cross
        when I am the broken

physics of desire
    trying to kiss
        my wife.

One

The man and the woman, his wife, are having it out on the couch.
He's pulled her whole body into him, is embracing her tightly, blindly,

and she's just torn gibberish, she's letting herself cry out of her lungs,
like a crushed flower, that he has *ruined* her, torched their marriage

by sleeping with the other woman at Starbucks, someone she knew
in passing, a woman who subbed at the tennis club. I listen to her

sobbing her pain into his shoulder, as if pain, too, could come to life
with its own bloodlust and passion, like one of the cut flowers in Eden.

The man is holding her, taking her woe into him, is sponging her pain.
I watch her arm curl around his neck, her silver bracelet dangling there

mid-arm like a shiny halo, where it slides down to her wrist and it lands,
lopsided, like a big ring — as if all wedding rings could somehow grow

more enormous with the years when two people love or hurt each other
with magnitude — and then, in time, the wedding ring can evolve

from the small novelty of its excited shining, there on the left finger,
and decidedly claim the whole wrist — as if love, utterly boundless,

must somehow get *larger,* more swelled with presence. I watch as her left leg,
long and sexy, bared now, lifts up with the other, half-hidden, right leg

to curl around him. She shoulders herself deeper into him, into his chest.
He's bewildered. I see it: his face gaunt and tortured, half-alive, half-gazing

out the window as she gives it to him again and again, the anguish she feels
at his betrayal. I almost get up, out of my chair, try to help him steady her

there as she rocks back into him. But instead, I move my face closer
to my coffee cup, inhale its deep aroma. Allow myself to drift backwards —

into my solitude again. Cars creep through the parking lot outside my window.
It's snowing. And the quiet hum of the heating vent drones

into the gentle room where we sit. Now she's at him again, trying to crawl
back into him. Into what must be his dark lost-and-found space in there.

That zone without any words that we all must hold inside us. That space
without any excuses, where the book we would write with one another

could suddenly burst open, a split binding, just a sheaf of bright pages,
blank and ready to write on with nothing else but the future in it —

that hopefulness — as if, because we are just heat and flame with one another
when we come together, we must somehow burn the other and then

be burned over again by the other until, unfazed, we become fazed again,
like fabric and needle with each other, stoked into rapture or in pained hurt

with the other again, so that the heat and the sudden flaring that we are
with each other could melt and join again, would merge, like a book

threading somehow in one flame, as if in the end we are nothing
but threads of eager flame. *One.* I watch, muted, keeping myself away

from how it is they must stitch up this transgression, this broken hem
of their love sickness. She grabs at his hand now, as if she's a lost

thread in search of a hem. She's a sewing needle, an eager flame.
And I watch him be sewed again, over and over until he, too,

feels the heat and the anguish of it, the love, the thread, the flame,
and they are one.

Roadside Gas Stop, Black Hills, South Dakota

The girl with the scar across her face from the fire
is singing at the top of her lungs about the policies

of the broken arrow. How the sacred pipe was
brought back to the people by White Buffalo Woman

after years of its absence because there had been
human sacrifice and the gasolining of the feminine

principle. All this in Rapid City, South Dakota,
where you can see the sacred buffalo hoarding

something of their mystery in silence among
the Black Hills. I want to howl for the policy of the

broken arrow, here at the counter of the Big D Oil Co.
where I see the boy flipping his brother off as they

page through motocross magazines while their
white daddy in his Stetson juices up the big F-150,

takes a big swig off the liquor bottle in his hand,
and smacks their mother across her forehead,

not once but three times, after she pulls open
his hunting jacket to get the cigarettes they share.

I want to howl at the top of my lungs for this one act
of ceremonial love and affection between them,

sing for their sacred tobacco, the hoop dance they do
for Wakan Tanka, for love of the poisoned lung,

for love of the medicine dance of self disgust
and the tablets they buy for someone's nausea.

I want to sing for the girl who has a scar on her face
as she rocks by herself holding Wakan Tanka's power,

sing for White Buffalo Woman and her sacred pipe,
sing for the rusted F-150 and the snow tires already

clanging beneath it across the exhausted blacktop.
I want to sing for the burned-out liability of people who don't

give a shit. Sing loudly for the Black Hills surrounding us
and the pine piedmont where, up-road, these people live.

Sing for the girl rocking herself to Wakan Tanka
and to White Buffalo Woman bringing blessings of beauty.

I want to sing for the trailer park and the medicine wheel
that it is, sing for the praising of valued items they break

in crowded quarters, bacon grease and splattered coffee
spread like engine oil across the kitchen counter. I want to

sing for the doorway that is opened, sing for the bundle
of child-woman holding her belly like it is sacred, sing for

the girl with the scar on her face rocking to Wakan Tanka's
power and to White Buffalo Woman's sacred pipe.

I want to sing for the rifles and guns in their trailer home
and all the angry buffalo roaming in it, and sing for their

fifteen-year-old daughter, alive and under the bed sheets,
a broken arrow, sick to her stomach, and pregnant.

Forgetting Is a Stone
Thrown into the Abyss by Memory

1.

Forgetting is a stone thrown into the abyss by memory.

That's why this baby, born here today in this sprawling hospital,
will forget the pump and thrust of his mother pushing him outwards

like her body carried tumultuous waves of sea water within it,

and so the birthing of this child became one wave after another,
hitting and crashing and thudding against the mother's pelvic floor,

until at last a child, a pink invited little collection of putty, appears;
and, out of nowhere, all the pain, all the ceaseless rocking, is forgotten,

and a mother holds a newborn child in her arms, because of it.

2.

Forgetting is a stone thrown into the abyss by memory,
and that's why this child, this ecosystem of resilience and recall,

will lose sight and sound of all this sea foam crashing into birth.

Knowing this, the soul, because it is vaporous and light, a love note,
belongs outside of time; it's within the realms of timelessness

maybe for an hour or so before it enters the long floral cavity
where birthing, because it's within the providence of all echoing, occurs.

Because of this, the mother, wild and sacrilegious in her desire
to bring this birthing child to being, gives up her hope to even live,

and that's why, after the birth, the mother's eyes curl upward,
small spinning rubies, and her hands claw at the bedsheets, for life.

3.

The baby, then, born because the soul inside it longs to witness
what happens to the color of the leaves on the spindly maple tree

growing outside the hospital birthing window, squiggles into waking,
and the mother, pale as fresh marble softened by scented oils,

giggles too, in response, because her soul, the one doing the birthing
here in the innocence of her flesh that's become minty with afterglow,

delights in something of the otherness of its making, which is close
to god, or divinity, whatever it is that the religious among us call it.

And the father, doing something clumsy with his bare hands, maybe
folding and unfolding the birthing towels, looks on, bewildered,

because the soul in him, a feckless rope unraveling out of slipknots,
feels vibrant and aroused, sort of like a dumb dog leaping at leaves,

although the man, unsure of himself, doesn't know where to put it,
his leaping confidence, and so he pats the bed four times, and he giggles.

4.

And because memory is the after-throw of the stone catapulting
into the abyss, the physician — the one whose hands engaged

this child wiggling itself into breathfulness — calls this child *a boy*,
as if the word "boy" could somehow catalogue the immense journey

of a sentient being, unnamable, steaming and kicking itself into breath.
And the parents, crazed by the bright metallic lights and the nurses

rushing in and out of the parade of their blue scrubs and shouting,
acknowledge this, *their son*, and they forget likewise the terms of birthing,

which is like the ocean frothing in a storm, and then from the tempest
and tumult comes forth a sleeping child, floating on a mother's belly.

I tell you, forgetting is a stone thrown into the abyss by memory.

And that's why, afterwards, after the sun has set, an amber glow,
the parents, resting together in this bed, their souls calmed, name the boy,

so that he, too — because he's a soul, just a feather of light breaded into form —
will forget himself for years; and then, at the edge of a maple tree,

maybe at this little one struggling bravely to keep its leaves by the hospital,
he will remember himself, wild and edgy, as someone from an abyss, born.

My Father's Trombone
Speaks to Me at the Winston Motel

All night I watched my father's labored breathing,
his drunken body like a slide trombone, gaunt and shiny,

his cheeks, caved in, defeated, his mouth, a wide bore hole
as he gasped, horned the hallow air out, sucked it deep

back in again, broken black-feathered birds choking his lungs,
while his trachea, like a telescopic slide,

moved and muscled breaths back and forth down tubular
throat stem while, beside him, on a small brown table,

the dozen bottles of liquor, the little green men, stood guard
watching him and me. Outside the cracked motel window

a couple argued, spat curses at each other, while the neon
sign blinked on and off, a consciousness flickering sickly,

and cars and trucks zoomed by. And as I sat there with him,
I counted his breaths, each a slide position on a trombone

with a particular song note, until I fell into a boy's dream.
And I heard my father's last six or seven breaths

gently escaping from him, the second breath from the last
being the final breath he'd take upon the release

of spirit—which would be that intrepid stardust breath,
that sentimental journey breath, that dipsy-doodle breath

bringing to bear the immaterial giveaway of soul purling free,
until the final breath, which would be the lowest

fundamental, the depressing of all the remaining
trombone valves—which I saw would be his freedom,

his death. And on the eighth breath I woke up, startled, alone,
caught in the silence of the room's blue pallor, and I felt

the traffic's distant drumming over the road outside the motel
rumbling me awake, and a person in the next room,

someone sleepless, moved from the window back to the chair
and turned the television volume up—it was a cigarette

commercial — while the sky outside broke soapy gray with dawn,
with birds and cars. And when my father woke up, his eyes

dim as porch lights in fog, his hair, spiked up, mud gray,
he took my hand, gently, he pulled me to him, me, his oldest

son, and he gathered to him all my longing, all my lost hours,
like he was collecting to him all the musical notes in me,

all the genetics of mine and his namesake, our same-names,
and he collected me into himself, into his Irish blood.

And he lit a cigarette like it was a tiny sun, something small
and heated he and I could smoke together so that it would

awaken us. And he confided in me that he'd dreamed I was
a seven-position trombone: my eyes full of golden sunlight,

my being full of energetic heraldry, my hands, firebrand finches
full of freedom, my spirit, a bursting brassiness, slender and dense

with bugle pronouncements, my body, all slide brass and cone,
lithe and green with eagerness to live, my mouth, a wide bore,

warm and rich with Irish laughter, with honking words of poetry
babbling forth, my young heart, melodic and soulful, a dark

muscle beneath sternum and rib, drowned in doubt — and I was
crushed and silent, a muzzled horn, until he woke up,

and he held me.

Oil-Covered Murre Washed Up on Garnet Sands

We were driving on the Pacific Coast Highway
    just south of Big Sur
        when we heard the news

that he had died. You'd pulled off to the highway edge
    where you waited while I slid down
        the dirt trail through a post-fire spectacular

of California poppy and purple needle grass.
    Below us, the ocean raged over gigantic rocks
        and a small gopher snake wiggled

under dry coyote bush and popcorn flower.
    Above us, Santa Lucia fir dominated the hillside.
        I worried that my knees would be scraped

as I fumbled down to the wet rocks drabbled purple-green
    with fingers of tangled marine algae,
        but I wasn't hurt. I was lucky because the trail,

massaged and protected by bush lupine and buckwheat
    and California sagebrush, was gentle, and pebbled
        with small here-and-there stones,

and below me, frothing with ocean surf and curtains of kelp,
    were the rocks of this private granite-altar cove
        where I stood watching the sunset.

And above me, I could see you looking down at me,
    trying to locate me,
        and I waved to you,

nearly slipping off the slimy rock into the sea ooze.
    Then, after, when the sunset fell
        and I saw the ocean steal all the light again

and seize it for the depths, for the blue nightfall,
    for the swelling surge of mindless waves
        overtaking all rock,

overtaking all else here on the intertidal zone,
    I thought of them,
        your father and mine —

men who still wore suit coats to eat dinner,
    men who had died, had left us years back;
        and I saw the oil-covered murre

washed up on the garnet sands of Big Sur —
    and he was lying there
        asleep in his white-and-black tuxedo,

a gentleman bird resembling a former butler
    or a concierge at a hotel or a state senator,
        someone regal, well-mannered,

and not of this impolite world any longer,
    someone like a relic, a personage
        no longer interested in this world —

dead here on the garnet sand, and he was beautiful
    and restful and still;
        and when I waved up

at you and I pointed to it,
    you waved back at me,
        at my life, as if you knew.

The Blue Violinist

— for Lance Wilcox

They were speaking strange words to each other one night
as we wandered behind them through the village after dinner,
our bellies rounded with wine, with after-dinner coffee,
for we were a young married couple, we were still in awe
with each other, with the picnic of our particular phrases
and meanings toward each other, whereas they were
clearly older, were obviously well past their dinner hour,
were working something out, something hurt between them out,
and she'd said to him, "you don't accept" — those were
her exact words to him — and he'd interrupted that allegation
for a quick instant, had griped about the humid night air,
about the density of crickets chirruping under bluebeard shrubs,
and about the ache in his left shoulder after swimming,
and in turn she'd said, "you don't, you know, *accept* —
you don't willingly, with a gentle grace, *own* something not *you*,"
she said, "you don't own my weaknesses like they are *yours*,
for instance, you don't *caress* them..." as if all that we present
to each other could be carried, would be assumed as a debt;
and he'd stopped, gauged that remark as it expanded in him,
while above us the blue violinist, floating in sweet surrealism
above the village, his face reddened by vivid charm, by laughter,
his legs crossed in idle joy in the chair, fiddled his barcarole,
painted it, really, like blue happy oxide all over the city,
all over the midnight blue of the rooftops and the cathedrals,
and the white bird, perched there on his high shoulder,
painted approximately the same exact color as the moon,
gossiped, babbled, warbled all the wandering love songs
that the ear and heart seem to need as we twist our head to listen,
as we attempt to talk with each other with ear and tongue
(because we are confessors with each other, we must listen);
and the blue violinist, floating and spinning himself around
and around in his wooden chair over the blue blush of city,
kept expanding over us, over our past, over our future,
over the attractions and wounds we all carry for each other,
as we walked hand in hand together into our uncertainties;
and the other bird, sitting on the blue violinist's knee, *wiggled*,
I swear it wiggled the way the blue heart wiggles, *crazily,* for love.

Devotion as the Aerobics of Love

Fireflies

On the outer edge of this faraway field, over a broken-down farm wagon,

above the wounded, mangled stump of a once-gigantic maple tree,

    amid a tangle of shrub thicket, green osier dogwood,

    and over the mottled stink and throaty belches of an inland swamp,

and across the way, among a brocade of forked apple trees in ruined orchard,

way down over yonder from an abandoned farmhouse, an American ruin

    whose windows crank emptiness, burnt indigo, painted night sky;

    and over its chimneys, where swallows explode by dusk, by dawn,

we raise our eyes, you and I, newly married, to the rising chimera of heaven

glowing on and off like strike-through light on an indigo coquille board;

    and we're caught in big blackness penetrated by crickets, coyotes,

    and nothing else we can identify except the mysteries of our future,

that Solomon's seal sketched over us body and soul, painted *sotto in su* —

    and we raise our eyes to the magical lights and demiglow tints that

    will guide us through our summers, fire our pupils with *heaven light,*

fireflies.

Bach's Little Anna Magdalena Book

— Prelude in C Major

"I will write for you *the music of your orgasms,*"
he whispered to her as they gazed up into

the plum-colored night sky to watch the stars;
"I will do this for you, you whose name means

'soprano at the gate with the voice of a meadowlark'..."
Keeping his delicate fingers arched over the keys

so as to be free to pass his thumbs beneath them
as he caressed in quick, sensual motion each key

of the harpsichord, each quill rising to pluck
the string above it, like gently striking at the edge

of her small earlobes so as to awaken the
meadowlarks she'd hear inside herself when

they made love, the composer moved steadfastly
to write each note — this as he did penance

for engaging in and playing unseemly variations
on the organ in a church, and this because he'd

served time in jail for an unruly dismissal, and this
because the angel Michael had visited Bach

one evening as the composer strolled alone
down cobblestone streets into a cayenne sunset,

each cloud a celery-colored hue, each building
toasted in a daffodil flambé, each new fugue

piling up like voices in conversation with each other,
like competing seagulls jeering in the wind, or

like a cluster of women harmonizing the vespers
beneath the arborvitae in delirium tremens

as they awaited the resurrection of their souls
to the gray watcher who stood lonesome at the lake,

and the angel had told Bach that he'd lose his eyes
because he was using the tips of each finger to *see* —

"and I will write for you these notes," he said again
to her, "until my fingers become red as strawberries

and until my eyes ignite, watching you, as you
raise each voice above the pedal point in you,

while you come."

Six Stanzas on the Soul

1.

Of all the places it could go, the soul, because it was forgetting
itself, went here, into our chests. Perhaps that was a mistake,
but, because the soul flies out like a bunch of grapes, what can I say —
it chooses the human body to dwell in. It gets stuck inside *us*.

Now and then, in distress, when we're crying over our heartbreaks,
the soul removes itself like a spiraling dragonfly,
and it settles somewhere, maybe on top of a glass bottle.
It waits us out, a bright idea hanging out on a limb,
until we're done expressing all of our turbulent glitter.

Then it leaps and zigzags, like a saffron finch.

2.

Lucretius, sitting on a stone slab, saw a bird electrify
into a billion bits of gold dust. That was the soul he saw.
And he saw it twisting around in the dirt.

The soul, a fraction of
memory, excites into particles — especially at the point
of dissolution. And so when a bird hunter looks up,
fires a shot and takes a duck down, Lucretius winks;
he sees a billion particles of *duck soul* scattering over
the ice-covered, tawny marshland.

Duck soul must look like a bunch of fat globules.

3.

Sometimes the soul, because it's of wanderlust, misses
its mark. Sometimes it lands outside of the chest,
and that's when some of the real trouble starts.

Marilyn Monroe's soul existed in her eyes.

Joe DiMaggio, because he couldn't understand the relationship
of soul to eyes, thought if he loved her *constantly*, she'd get well.

Nobody whose soul is in the eyes gets better. That one's fatal.

Hitler's soul — well, that's an easy one. It landed in his mind,
where corruptibility is at its most agitated. When the soul's
landlocked in the mind, you get a megalomaniac.

I think Sigmund Freud's soul got stuck in his pecker.

4.

Because Jesus is a metaphor for the soul, artists paint it as a child.
That's why the Dutch painters paint the Madonna as God's lover.

In Jan van Eyck's *The Virgin and Child with Canon van der Paele,*
you see the Virgin, too. She's gazing away from the Christ child —
that pink little crocus that's blooming in her lap — because she
feels the Godhead's vibration, the Him, about to sprawl...

The soul is like blue water waves. It sprawls. That's what surfing's about.
That's what Brian Wilson, because he was losing his mind, wrote about.

Can you imagine the young Dylan — riding cross-country in the back
of a station wagon in '64, writing "Chimes of Freedom" —
how it was when he remembered being under a cathedral's tolling bells
and hearing "the chimes of freedom flashing"?

       The soul *is* a flashing.

5.

Or here's Plotinus on the soul: the One and the Nihil are the same.

That's a good one, because the Latin poets write of it, too.

Can you imagine Neruda wrestling with Plotinus? Well, that
one's literature, because in the odes, where the Nihil and the One
sleep together, there's a saffron finch.

And that's the soul, wrestling with space, time, all the imaginables.
And then, there's the *after* space, the unimaginable,
where once the soul *leaves* you, you can't touch it...
Because it's gone. Over the mountains. Over the sea.

Though you dream of it and it enters you again; it's interchangeable.

And that's Plotinus: One and Nothing are the same.

6.

Neruda's soul, well, that one's true. His soul was transferable.
It was like one of his finches. It leapt out of him, into his women,
into those great poetic lines. Into immortality.
You can't subtract what it is, though,
that *essence,* that saffron finch,
because it's some of the firelight you carry,
and it wears your name for something like 80 years
before it's gone again, nameless, into the ethers.

Once, in remorse, Neruda called that finch —
his metaphor for his own imperfect humanity,
a pitiful handful of extinguished feathers —
and the light of it left a pile of smoldering sunbeams.

The body's a pitiful handful of extinguished feathers...

This is Neruda busy handwriting at his table,
a bowl of fresh grapes, picked at, beside him,
the finches going at it like wild in the trees...
And the soul's a bowl of scintillant sunbeams.

In between them, something like grace, poetry, life.

Riccioli & the Seas of the Moon

Look here at this picture: It is Riccioli, the Italian Jesuit,
gazing at a young nun, a white blossoming moonflower
stretching her naked arms beneath the dark skies of Bologna
as the prostitutes and their drunken men bump and grind
against the flat sides of the soiled buildings, while the moon,
serene up above them, glistens and shines with its veiled
landscapes of light and shade becoming clear moving seas.

God will tell me, he thinks, what it is I should do with it,
this moon bursting above me like a baptized plum.
God will tell me what it is I should do with this young nun.

She is only fifteen, he thinks, and old enough to have
felt her menses move with the moon. The seas move
within her. Something of her soul is filled up with the chalice
of God, and there is a movement inside himself that he
can't seem to detect with his pendulum, nor can Grimaldi,
the both of them gazing downward in thought
as they pass the young nun by, through the 666 arches
of the Portico San Luca, on their way back to the Asinelli Tower.

God will tell me what to do with her, this moonflower
stretching herself awake beneath the city tower.
God will tell me, because He is a mysterious hoot owl,
and I am a disciple of torment and love, which is the moon.

Now, later on in his observatory, Riccioli, smitten by
this young nun stretching herself under the big sky,
begins to describe the names of the moon's landscape:
Listen to their names: *the sea of clouds, the sea of storms,*
the sea of nectar, the sea of moisture, the sea of crisis,
the serpent sea, the sea of fertility, the foaming sea...
Listen to the names he gives to the moon's surface.
Listen to the names he gives that act for the ages.

Django Reinhardt, I Saw Stars

— a guitar has moonlight in it
— James M. Cain

On stage in 1934, in a Paris club
with the *Quintette du Hot Club de France,*

the opening piano, flirting, tickling
the whole crowd into foot-tapping,

and Stephane Grappelli zigzagging
on his violin through the dim heat

of the club, the band seductively takes up
"I Saw Stars," and Reinhardt, his two

burned fingers the color of gray trout,
moves up and down the neck of the guitar

like a gypsy boy foot-tapping
through the Romani gypsy camps.

His name, Django, means "I awaken,"
and as Grappelli heats up the violin strings

with gaiety, Django's cells are flooded
with florescence and falling zodiacs,

as if music, because it is constructed
of dancing gypsies, fireballs and flowers,

is somehow born of gaiety and fire,
of excitement, as if it is hyperactive,

something driven by campfires, heat,
gypsy banjos, and firework fingering.

Now Reinhardt, awake, ignites
the fire-starting mechanics of the guitar

as the patrons of the club — verdant,
multicolored flowers flaring in blaze —

bob their heads up and down,
fists raised in jubilation as if they're on fire,

and Grappelli, stirred into campfire
heat with it, twists it, turns it, vaults

the music upward, which provokes
Reinhardt into beating the guitar strings

with the matchsticks of his right fingers,
lighting it on fire, really, so that the song

resembles a dancing campfire cooking up
the gypsy moonlight, creating stars.

Someone in the audience, a woman,
laughs, claps her excited hands loudly,

and the silver bracelets dangling
from her thin wrist resemble celluloid paper,

one of the shiny celluloid flowers that Bella
would patiently create for the street sales

back home in the gypsy encampment,
and the bracelet flashes, almost as if it's

a bursting star, which stirs Reinhardt
into a reactive excitement, as if music,

the entangled, delirious flickering of it
in his two fingers, could become a lit torch

stirring each note into a streak of firelight
darting down fret and over the gaping hole

of the guitar, so as to fill it up —
the deep dark drowned pit of it

where all the awe and terror is —
with music, with stars.

The Wizard of Oz & Dorothy

"Our wishes, do you think they ever go away?"
he asked her while pulling a cigarette out of his
expensive suit coat pocket and lighting it casually.
This was just yesterday and I was listening to them,
reading my book on sex and love, 1900 to present.
He caught her red pump in his loafer and they
rocked quietly together, not really flirting, for he
was much older than her and she was still a girl.
And the young woman answered politely, earnestly,
"They stay in the eyes; you can tell in the gaze,
even in the old people, you can tell if their wishes
are still there." And the man, talking to the girl
while pointing at the white-scented pond lily
and the group of ducks wiggling around it, said,
"The world is full of those who pick a handful
of wildflowers to give away, and then there are
those who let them stay planted where they are.
And then there are those who will pick the flowers
just to get them for themselves, and that's greed.
Don't walk with them, do you hear me, don't do it."
She nodded absently, feeling something in her eyes
twitter and something in her heart twist up.
"Do you believe wishes are just illusions?" he asked her.
"Oh no, I don't think so; I hope not," she answered
while ruffling her skirts and crossing her legs and
looking over a small bruise on the top of her leg
and then taking a smoke for herself. "I truly
believe in the idea of a rainbow; and you can
spend a lifetime trying to get over it, don't you think?
That's not greedy, is it?" she asked again, more
curious than convinced of what she was saying.
And he, "Well, if the dreams you dare to dream
for yourself really do come true, then it must be so."
She smiled a smile as large as a clarinet. Sighed.
Let her wandering eyes fix on a young sailor pushing
himself against a woman under a big tree.
"I think I will write a song for you to sing," he said.
And then he stretched his arm across her shoulder,
pulling her into him like she was a vaudeville orphan.

Large passenger balloons floated over the wide area.
He pointed them out to her, said, "look over there."
Some landed, some kept on floating over the city.
One of them landed nearby the large willow trees.
"How strange it must be when an illusion dies..."
she said out loud to the open air full of buzzing bees.
"It's as though you've lost a child," she spoke again.
He stroked her hair just then, said, "Don't think of it...
I'll always be here for you, over there, where blue
birds fly." And he pointed out the canopy of willow trees
growing in front of the city to the west of the park,
and how it was that a clever idea could conceal the cruel
world and show us the emerald world in front of it —
the world of lemon drops high above the chimney tops,
he hummed to her, pointing to edge if the sky line.
"Somewhere, over the rainbow, way up high..." he sang.
Let himself wrap the melody around the words.
Touched her on the chin and looked into her eyes.
Felt the strangest urge to kiss her on the mouth.
"I've just had the strangest sense of it," she said,
ruffling her skirt again and twisting to face him.
"How one can be so very lost, so very taken away..."
"Into one's wishes you mean?" he asked her,
"is that it?" And her, "No, it's more than that..."
"Into others' wishes," she said then, gravely. "Into other
peoples' wishes for you." Traffic roared. Busses,
taxis, and a group of schoolgirls ran up to her.
One of them almost touched her on the cheek.
"You have the shiniest red shoes on!" the girl exclaimed.
The wizard bent over, tapped Dorothy's red shoe,
said, "These will take her up over the rainbow."
And Dorothy clicked her red shoes, eyes closed,
felt the wind in her wishes, lifting them away.

Andrea Amati & the Creation of the Violin

Underneath the rose window of the Cathedral of Cremona,
he is struck by the shape of the shin-bone volute,

that small exotic seashell found on the beaches of Japan,
which an artist has sketched for him because it resembles

the body of woman he knows lying serene on a divan.
And this, because Amati has become enchanted

by the way the human voice is but the hark and hallelujah
back to heaven in prayer. And this because Amati

is in love with a woman whose body mimics the structure
of a shin-bone volute, which is a shell with wide hips

and a throat slender enough to hold a streak of songbirds
inside it who glide from flower to flower in prayer

and who sing all the moments of rapture into the wind.
And this, because Amati has been called by God to make a violin.

God appears to Amati as a dead bird near the cathedral
whose broken body, lying there on the cobblestone street,

is stiff and browned by the day, and so the violin maker
is inspired to bring back to life the human longing for God

inside the breastplate of an instrument, which God tells Amati
will be the way we'll push holy praise and *vox humana*

through the arc and stretch of song, which will be the violin,
which is, itself, the body of man and woman here on earth,

with sloping shoulders and curved waist, and a hole in the gut
made deep with loneliness and the wellspring of prayer.

And so he carves the wood into a musical instrument
and he strings a bow with the hair of a horse, which is the male

animal God placed in front of the chariots of fire
that carry all the souls backwards and forward to heaven.

This, Amati thinks, will be the lifted structure and voice
of the human heart singing a way back to heaven,

and so he carves it, shapes it into a body just like ours,
polishes it so that its wooden shoulders feel as smooth

as human skin, and he gives it the name *violin* —
which means "make a path back to God."

One Angel, Listening to Mozart & Seeking Her Birth, Goes Free

— for Joy Gaines-Friedler

The angels, gathered together under the green cypress trees
and listening to Mozart's Violin Concerto #1 in B-flat major,

were arguing among themselves on what color to be
as they took on human form. The one with the large flea eyes

had said "bluegum eucalyptus," whereas another had argued
for the red of the western bleeding heart, and another still

had held forth for the mottled flecks of white alder bark.
"The skin of the human is *imperfect,* like the flecks of an alder,"

he'd said, "whereas all the other colors are just encaustic wax
on the realms of glamour." This said, the angels became

irresolute and agitated as they watched the men streaking
in swarms below on the streets of Vienna at Christmastime

and, among them, all the ladies adorned in lights. The violins
of Mozart's concerto, which God had told the angels

to listen to as the singular force of rapture that celebrates
how nothingness turns to new life on an umbilical string,

played on through the muted stillness of the cypress trees.
All this as God looked on from a swathe of operatic silence.

"Love is a *portent of emotional strength,*" the one angel, stroking
himself like an entangled moonbeam, said, and the other,

dressing himself up as a western pasqueflower, argued that
"beauty is based on frequency invariance, a continuity of form,"

whereas giving over to one's death is like an anthem to God,
which is, he argued, "rapture, transcendence." The one girl

angel among them, herself a rubberlip seaperch, swept herself
aside like an incessant, restless mesmerism with bee-wing fins,

and she fell upon a great rock in the middle of the glade and said,
"the soul coming into life on earth is a violin cutting itself a place

through beauty invariance and *all* the frequencies, which is *birth —* "
and, exhausted by the loss of air from her lungs, yelled in gasps, "*I'm free.*"

Devotion Is the Aerobics of Love

— for Bradley Spencer & Jane Durand

I'm a man standing at the Book of Love,
    writing Inscriptions in it.

I believe the best virtue to carry to Love's Altar
    is a steadfast Curiosity —

bathed in a Genteel Humanity.
    Everything you learned

in Boy Scouts applies. Strength of Purpose helps —
    it's Attractive.

So is a well-balanced Magnetism.
    I've capitalized certain words in this poem

because I believe in Emily Dickinson.
    Occasionally humor helps

when you've messed up with a woman,
    but sincerity works best.

Being in awe of a woman is a trap,
    I've found, but being Irreverent

is its own stupidity. Watching your step
    is foolish, but step-watching is wise.

A woman is another country and so is a man.
    That's the best premise point

to begin with. One plus one equals two
    and then you get three,

which is a Marriage, which is, itself,
    yet another Country that two

must walk sure-footed in.
    It has a yellow brick road in it —

and flying monkeys, witches and wizards
    in it too. Strange governors

that get elected and then, just as quickly
    as that, dismissed.

It holds a History in it that is
        seductive and important and then,

just as quickly as the pages of it blurring,
        irrelevant and limiting.

It also has lush Emerald Meadows
        and Pots of Rainbows.

Having fun in it is less important
        than learning the rules of fun.

And then, having fun in it is essential.
        Sex works best when the focal point

is Rapture with Lust as lubricant.
        There are Gods and Goddesses.

They live inside us. It's best to drink
        deeply from their chalice.

And don't get caught up with male
        and female terminology.

Androgyny works best — because we
        are rays of theatrical light

mixing together, which is Intercourse.
        Other than that,

Devotion is the aerobics of love.
        Practice it daily.

Open your lungs up to it
        so that one day you can

explode back into it —
        into that other source

from which the stream
        of Intending first came.

The Angel in the Mouth

— for Jeff Alfier & Tobi Cogswell

A long time ago, before television
stole the angel and computers —
specifically the Internet, rendered
it insignificant — there was an angel,
soft as a mint leaf, that lived
at the edge of the tongue where it
narrowed, turned into a tip.
At the tip of the tongue, where
the garden of delight grows
or is contaminated by envy,
the angel lived in a globe of spit
like a little fairy, and it would
come awake during courtship,
whenever there was the insight
of beauty, the touch of the tongues,
the fragrance of Eros and Agape.
It was here that beauty, by way
of court and spark, flowed
between the lovers, and the voice,
which was the song of the angel
beating her wings into ecstasy,
became the call that joined us as one.

During the quarrels between lovers
that characterized the 20th Century —
and I mean those quarrels that
split the sexes into a crude contest
of wills and genital divisions —
the angel would startle awake,
almost like a small fruit fly, and it
would fly out of the mouth, wings
aflutter, and awaken the two
quarreling beings.
Those that were awakened well,
like D. H. Lawrence for instance,
declared love as the route home
again. And those who refused
the angel created this ceaseless
pursuit of the angel's impostors,

which are the realms of glamour
that we see in the catalogs
and on the porn sites showing men
and women as playthings
and not as inviolable souls, or as bees
seeking what it is the honey's for.

  You can see the mint angel
in the early photographs of the last
century. She is that unexplainable
glow, that smudge of light
behind someone's head.
Photographers have explained this
away as camera lens phenomena or
exposure problems. But the angel
in the mouth, which is part of the
21 grams we're missing at death,
is really there. She's like a dental light.
Like the heat in the blood-furnace
burning its light in the iris.

  When you are awakened
by the angel, you feel the DNA
of your body being invaded by a
soul-dancing. Your eyelids flutter,
as if congruent with its wings,
and you remember that you are here
to sing the story of the tongue
and its words as they unwind into form
between you and someone you love,
and you forget what it is you
are arguing for. The Spanish poets
know of the angel, especially
Jiménez, who notes that the
angel is like "the water that
goes from flower to flower,
like a butterfly that sings."

The Waves Carry Our Names in the Stars Forever!

She shouted out to him, close in his ear,
    madly in love now
        or drunk as they raced in the convertible,

top down and speeding around the coastal roads
    to the crazed sea where the waves
        (they could hear them crashing steadily)

were sandbagging the beach below.
    They could hear the waves tumbling
        like drunken Knights of the Round Table

as if trying to find the sturdy shore again,
    their safe kingdom,
        as if they'd become somehow lost at sea,

enraptured by the way they could swim and swim forever
    and never arrive home,
        because the waves have shiny stars, lovers,

dancing beyond them, and it is a form of sea blindness.
    The kids, dizzy, fell to their knees
        once they reached the beach.

Something inside the boy felt completely free.
    Like he'd reached a place he couldn't rightly name.
        Some exalted expanse without borders.

The girl gripped him then, pulled him back to her body.
    He felt her heavily breathing there,
        clutching him close.

And the surging waves were lost, too,
    in the mesmerizing oceanic darkness
        where the light, sometimes, was just a visitor.

She wasn't seventeen yet, and he was just eighteen,
    and they were a couple
        and they were madly in love,

which is a wishing spell, something tentative
    and then frenetic all at once,
        that overtakes all of the willing victims,

all of us spell seekers,
    all of us who are lost at sea
        with the sea blindness.

And the sea blindness, the love sickness,
　　　　was brought forth to them,
　　　　　　　like it is in all of us, by the bright stars

falling down over us and into our soul cages
　　　　in spells of mystery and exalted commotion.
　　　　　　　And it was brought forth, too,

like it always is by the daemon, the love angel of devastation
　　　　lurking there in the wild, lusty pine trees
　　　　　　　way up on the ridge

where the two kids had held onto each other's bodies,
　　　　and they'd breathed their lovemaking breaths
　　　　　　　at once together like two churches,

like the two pearly everlasting altars that they were.
　　　　And it was brought forth, too,
　　　　　　　by the weird, unknown world

inside of them, unknown to all of us, too —
　　　　because it comes through the veil of forgetting,
　　　　　　　which is also a swirling sea —

and it is a strange loop and a lostness and a déjà vu.
　　　　And later on, by the wooden boat
　　　　　　　that had capsized on the shore,

the one drowned by kelp strands and by all other
　　　　manner of sea dressing,
　　　　　　　she wrote her name excitedly

on the sand for him inside a curved heart-shape
　　　　she'd sketched with a stick.
　　　　　　　Said her name was in the stars above

so he'd never forget her. Said it must be the way
　　　　the heart reaches out or in, but she didn't know
　　　　　　　why she said it.

Mostly, though, it felt like she was becoming glitter.
　　　　Something of the deep sea was pulling her back out or in.
　　　　　　　She said to him,

"remember me for always," for he was leaving her
　　　　for college. And he grabbed the stick from her,
　　　　　　　held onto it like a rope, something stiff

yet noodled and wet because it broke easily in his hand,
　　　　salted and waterlogged as it was.
　　　　　　　And they wrestled somehow

for something unforgettable in the waves, for the world
        that was or wasn't quite a part of them yet.
                For everything else, too,

that was dividing them when they couldn't handle it.
        And they wrestled all across the wet beach
                until they were tired and itching,

then they lay down together, quiet as small diamonds of light
        snuggled down into a pit. She put her big eyes
                all over him. Sent her starlight into his iris.

He felt it. Held onto it like it was a glowing comet—
        a dancing star, named, alive there.
                And another wave charged the shore

behind them—it crashed, it fell, it stumbled—exhausted.
        And she couldn't see it, for it fell back there,
                behind her, along the rim of the shore.

But he twisted back to gaze at it. And he saw the stars above it
        shattering over the sea like silver comets.
                Like handfuls of jewelry, glitterball globes.

So much beautiful starlight, with so many glowing globes
        breaking over the water—over his wide-open heart—
                he couldn't even count them all.

Acknowledgments

Grateful acknowledgment is made to the following publications in which these poems first appeared, some in slightly different versions.

A Narrow Fellow: "Learning to Taste the Chocolate," "Matinee"
Birdfeast: "Roadside Gas Stop, Black Hills, South Dakota"
Boxcar Review: "The Blue Violinist"
Burningwood Literary Journal: "Three Birds Orchid"
Chaffin Journal: "Devotion Is the Aerobics of Love," "Forgetting Is a Stone Thrown into the Abyss by Memory"
Concho Review: "Ricciolli & the Seas of the Moon," "The Wildest Girls"
Controlled Burn: "Django Reinhardt, I Saw Stars"
Kestrel: "My Father's Trombone Speaks to Me at the Winston Motel"
Lake Effect: "My Fingers Move Across the Typewriter Keys in an Effort to Find You," "Sister Kathleen Ann"
Muddy River Poetry Review: "Andrea Amati & the Creation of the Violin," "One Angel, Listening to Mozart & Seeking Her Birth, Goes Free"
Otis Nebula: "I Am Not the Composer of Poetic Reverie Anymore," "She Was Caressing Me"
Pea River Journal: "Pictures"
Pirene's Fountain: "Bach's Little Anna Magdalena Book," "My Wife & I"
Rattle: "Psych Ward," "Strip Clubs, Tampa," "Woman Releasing a Tongueless Swallow from Her Violin"
River Oak Review: "Reading Piaget w/Margo," "Six Stanzas on the Soul," "Some Purple Violets at the Market"
Ruminate Magazine: "Oil-Covered Murre Washed Up on Garnet Sands"
San Pedro River Review: "Concerning the Metaphysics of My Wife's Otherness," "Empathy," "Fireflies," "The Girls at the Vista Maria Home for Truants"
Sierra Nevada College Review: "On Highway 90, in South Dakota, Margo & I See in the End What We Become"
Skidrow Penthouse: "The Wizard of Oz & Dorothy"
Spillway: "1991 at the Movies"
Sulphur River Literary Review: "My Wedding"
Temenos: "The Angel in the Mouth"
The Dunes Review: "Adolescence"
Third Wednesday: "Forgiving," "One," "Some Young Men Undressing"

Cover artwork, "Wasserschlangen II (Freundinnen)," by Gustav Klimt; author photo by Margo Scott-Meisel; cover and interior book design by Diane Kistner; Book Antiqua text and Italianno titling